Book #3 in the Bro-Peep Funny Rhyming Adventure Series

Peep's Big Dig!

Written by Linda Denning
Illustrated by Gustyawan
Edited by Emily Denning

Published in Southaven, MS

Printed in United States of America

Library of Congress Control Number: 2025904670

ISBN:

Paperback 978-1-965992-90-6

Hardcover 978-1-965992-91-3

Dedicated to Sophia, Daniel, and Nathan, three brave little adventurers.

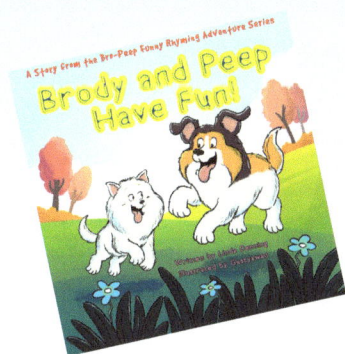

A Story from the Bro-Peep Funny Rhyming Adventure Series

Brody and Peep Have Fun!

Written by Linda Denning
Illustrated by Jelena Ivetkovic

Peep tried to act as puppies should.
She truly wanted to be good.

Peep had one fault–but it was big.
That little puppy loved to DIG!

No one could ever really guess
How much she loved to make a MESS!

DON'T DIG THERE, PEEP!

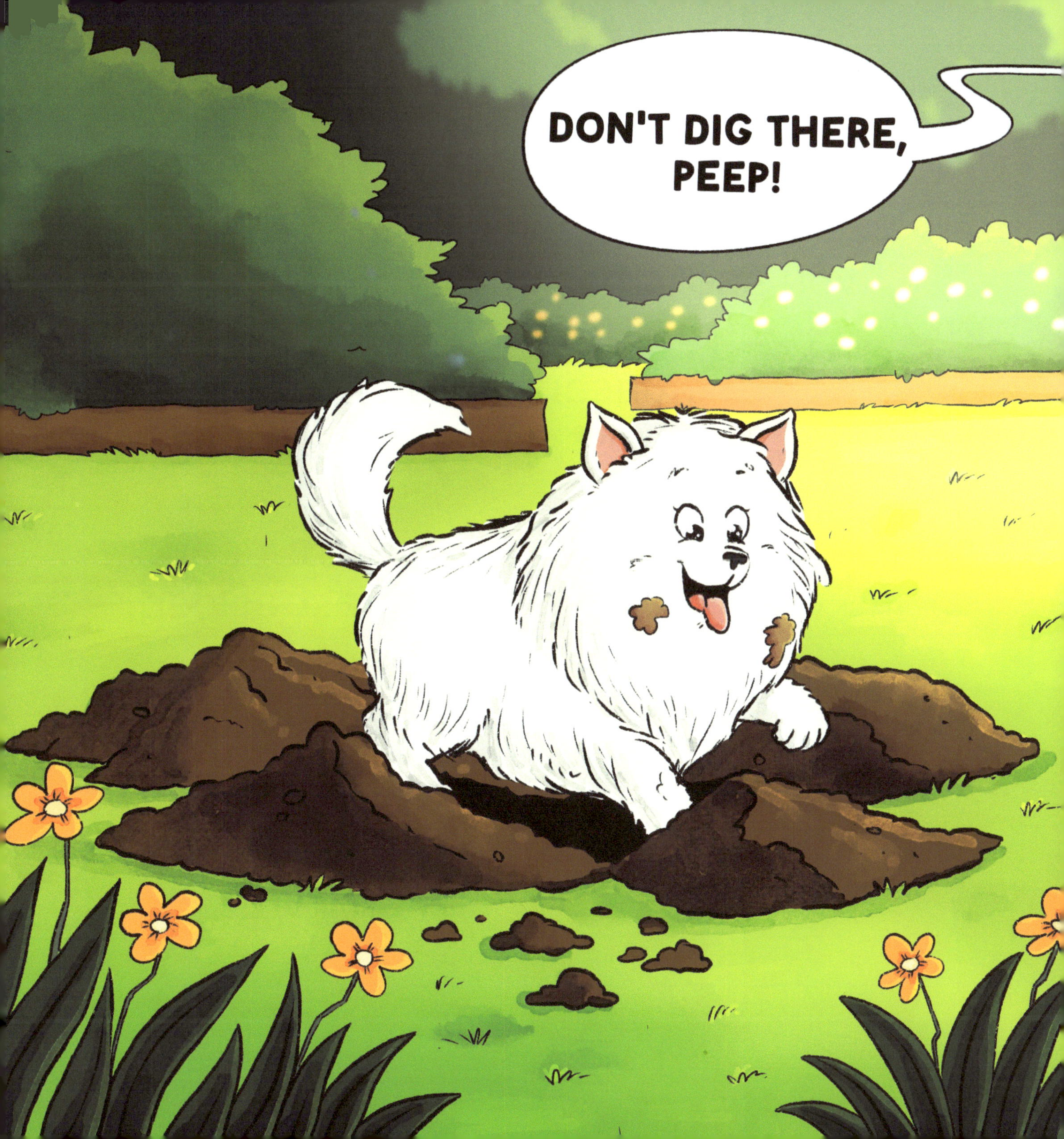
DON'T DIG THERE, PEEP!

Peep digs deep holes extremely well–
all you see is her fluffy tail.

When Peep unearthed a sleeping frog,
It said, "Get lost, you nosy dog!"

When Peep was digging extra deep,
She found some bunnies fast asleep.

A rabbit told that naughty pup,
"Paws out! You'll wake my babies up!"

DON'T DIG THERE, PEEP!

And when not busy digging rocks,
Peep played in Mittens's litter box.

She pawed the sand,
then kicked some more,
And kicked that litter on the floor.

The heaps of sand filled up their home
while Peep dug like a messy gnome.

The sand piles made Peep's family screech,
"Our house looks like a dirty beach!"

DON'T DIG THERE, PEEP!

Peep found a bone! It was not hard.
Dug from another dog's backyard.

Peep thought this new game so much fun
She soon swiped bones from everyone!

Brody tried to give some advice
To make that naughty Peep think twice,

"You'd better leave those treats alone.
It's wrong to steal another's bone."

DON'T DIG THERE, PEEP!

They heard a noise and peeked outside.
A pack of angry puppies cried,

"Your digging makes us really mad.
We know that you've been bad bad BAD!

"You took our bones and that's not right.
Give them back or we'll bark all night!"

Peep passed bones back and made amends.
The other dogs became her friends.

DON'T DIG THERE, PEEP!

When Dad came out to mow the lawn,
He saw that it was almost gone!

Deep holes as far as he could see
And mud where he thought grass should be.

"That's it!" Dad cried, "Peep's on a roll!
She's wrecked the yard. She's not a mole!"

DON'T DIG THERE, PEEP!

Though she liked having muddy paws,
Peep tried to keep the puppy laws.

Brody said, "Don't make a sad face!
I know the perfect digging place.

"When people dig, they find a mine.
There's one close by. I've seen the sign.

"Let's go, my favorite digging pup!
This time, there's nothing to mess up."

DIG HERE, PEEP!

Red dirt as far as Peep could see–
A digging puppy's fantasy.

That dog got started right away.
She hopped straight in and yelled, "Hooray!"

Nothing was safe from fluffy paws.
She made dirt fly with tiny claws.

DIG HERE, PEEP!

Her family dug with shovels and picks,
But could not match Peep's puppy kicks.

Working hard, there was no contest–
Peep dug more holes than all the rest.

She saw a sparkle in the ground–
the largest crystal ever found!

DIG HERE, PEEP!

Brody could not believe Peep's luck,
and thought they'd need a moving truck.

A rock that big would weigh a lot!
More than a car! More than a yacht!

DIG HERE, PEEP!

A different dog came home that day
Caked head to toe in bright orange clay.

With head held high, Peep understood
Her love for digging could be good.

If you love a job and do it well,
Be proud and wag your puppy tail!

DIG HERE, PEEP!

Mittens saw Peep and shook her head.
She turned up her small nose and said,

"Welcome back, my dirty buddy.
Take a bath, for you're all muddy!"

GO TO SLEEP, PEEP!

If you keep digging, bear in mind,
You never know what you might find.

A treasure or a hidden clue
A marvel waiting just for you.

But do not pick just any space–
You have to dig in the RIGHT PLACE!

DIG HERE, PEEP!

The End

Did You Know?

You can visit a crystal mine! Grab a bucket and head to Mt. Ida, Arkansas, quartz crystal capital of the world. At some of the mines, you can even bring your pup, so go find some treasure!

Visit www.lindadenning.com to learn more about digging for quartz crystals.

www.ingramcontent.com/pod-product-compliance
Lightning Source LLC
LaVergne TN
LVHW072059070426
835508LV00002B/181